My family weekend
Fun and Learn
Shapes

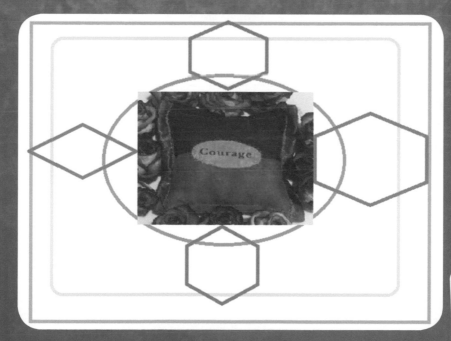

REHANA AKHTER

ISBN: Softcover   978-1-7960-5306-7
        EBook   978-1-7960-5305-0

Print information available on the last page

Rev. date: 08/23/2019

To order additional copies of this book, contact:
Xlibris
1-888-795-4274
www.Xlibris.com
Orders@Xlibris.com

My family weekend
Fun and Learn Shapes

Author: Rehana Akhter

Illustrator: Rehana Akhter

Star

The star is made out of wooden sticks.

There is also an orange inside this star.

Can you count how many total numbers of wooden sticks are used to make this star?

Heart

How many wooden sticks do you see?

Triangle

This shape is made out of 11 oranges.

The leaves on the oranges are green.

Circle

Can you tell me how many wooden sticks
are used to make this Circle?

How many oranges are there in total?

Square

All four sides are equal.

I have used 8 oranges and 8 wooden sticks to make this Square.

8 + 8 =

How many sides does a Square have?

Rectangle

Rectangle opposite sides are equal.

Can you count how many oranges were used to make this Rectangle?

Diamond

Four wooden sticks and four oranges were used to make this Diamond shape.

4 + 4 =

Oval

Can you count how many Oranges are there?

Pentagon

How many angles does a Pentagon have?

How many oranges are there?

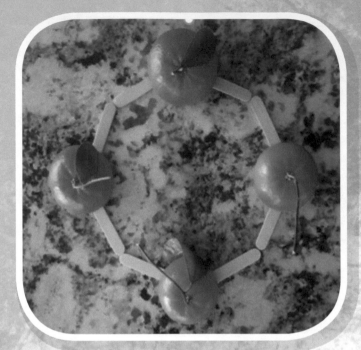

Octagon

Octagon has 8 sides and 8 angles.

How much is 8 + 8 =

Hexagon

How many angles does a hexagon have?

How many oranges are there?

This book sends a message to the parents and the new writers to encourage teaching kids in a unique way. Also, it gives idea to parents to create the shapes with their kids' favorite items. More importantly, spend quality time and have fun with their kids.

My younger daughter Alaina Zaman and my son Zada Zaman's favorite fruit is orange.

That's why I decided to make shapes with them using oranges. They learned the name of the shapes and how to count numbers by counting the oranges and the wooden sticks.

This book is dedicated to my three kids, Alvina Zaman, 5th grade, Zade Zaman, 2nd grade, Alaina Zaman Pre K and my parents, Khudeja Begum and Ishaque Khan.

CPSIA information can be obtained
at www.ICGtesting.com
Printed in the USA
BVHW021931080919
557875BV00002B/29/P